Chap

MW01221665

Intro: A Note from the Author

This is a devotional *for* teens, written *by* a teen. My name is Abby Mannion, and I am currently 16 years old. I live an average life. I love to write, and so here I am writing to you about different aspects of living life as a follower of Jesus Christ. First of all, I want to say that I'm nowhere near perfect. I don't have all the answers, and I am simply an ordinary girl. I am a sinner who has been saved and cleansed by the grace of God alone. I do not write to condemn you or to tell you how you should live your life. I am simply writing because God has laid it on my heart to do so; this is something I'm passionate about, and these are ideas I want to share with you. I write based on what God has taught me in my own experiences and through His Word, and I write as a friend and sister in Christ.

The way in which you choose to read this devotional is totally up to you. It's not necessarily meant to be a "daily" devotional. I would actually recommend spending several days on each chapter. I encourage you to pick apart each chapter, and really think over the context, reviewing it for several days.

Some chapters have many scripture references. I would also encourage you to not just read the verses referenced, but to actually look up each verse in your Bible. Maybe you could even write out the different verses and hang them around your room, or put them on notebooks that you use. Instead of just skimming the verses once, take the time to write them out and read over them. This practice will help you to truly hide them in your heart.

These are obviously just recommendations. I hope and pray that you are able to get something out of this devotional - not because of anything I've done or written, but because God is working in your heart.

<u>Chapter 1: More Than Motions</u>

Do you feel like your spiritual life has just consisted of unfulfilling, empty rituals?

Learn:

Christians often get stuck in a rut; it's the rut of "going through the motions," and we all have trouble getting out of it. This seems to be a very big issue, especially in our generation. I would define "going through the motions" as practicing the basic actions a Christian "should" do without really applying or learning anything from them or being strengthened by them. It's the idea of saying you're a Christian and knowing in your heart that you love God and want to serve Him, but at the same time carrying this heavy feeling of lacking true fulfillment in that relationship.

You go throughout every day the same exact way. God becomes a minor priority and is often pushed to the side. You attend church and youth group and occasionally send up a quick prayer or two, and the feeling of spiritual dryness and general unfulfillment still follows close behind you. There's a lacking of excitement, of true joy, and – most importantly – of the "fire" that you once experienced in your spiritual walk. And, quite frankly, there is a basic lack of God in your life in many ways.

I have been down this path many times. When I've caught myself walking the path of purely going through the motions, I often find that I become very confused and frustrated. I get confused about why I can't seem to "connect" with God more, and I end up blaming Him for the distance and the unfulfillment that I feel. ***Everyday becomes a monotonous cycle of events in which there seems to be no real purpose***. Can you relate to my experience?

Here's what I've learned about this feeling of being stuck in the motions:

1. It's a good thing to realize that you're only going through motions and not full-heartedly pursuing Christ. However, it's the decisions you make *after* you come to this realization that are going to change how you live (or not change anything).

2. No one is forcing you to walk this path. It's your choice whether you keep walking in the monotony and unfulfillment of the empty motions or whether you seek something more substantial.

3. Getting off the path of going through the motions will require sacrifice, but through the sacrifice will come blessings, joy, and renewed life.

4. God is by your side all the time and there is purpose in *everything* you do. Keeping your relationship with Him a priority will give you insight into the rest of life's meaning and will give you the motivation you need to live life well!

Act:

I'm going to take these four ideas listed above and apply them to the actions you can take to get off this unproductive, unfulfilling path. Going through the motions can be become a habit that is hard to break, and the first thing to understand is that you absolutely cannot change this habit by your own strength. Getting off this path requires complete trust in God because you are moving from something that is very comfortable into a new realm that is unknown.

Let's talk about the first and second points from the list above. What do you do after you realize that you've been walking the empty path of motions? What kinds of decisions do you have to make to get off this path and onto the path of true life?

Well, it's going to look a little different for each person because we're all unique. However, there are two very basic things that you can do. This may seem like a typical Sunday school answer...do you know where I'm going with this? The two things that every person should do are pray and read the Bible. Very basic, right?

It's true that these action steps are basic in the sense that they are simple. However, they are also very powerful. Doing these two things consistently and on a daily basis can literally change your life and are very key elements to living a life of real spiritual growth and fulfillment. If being stuck in the motions is something you're struggling with, then it is very possible that you have not been consistent in doing these two basic things. I know this is very true of me. Every time I feel like I'm just going through the motions, I catch myself practicing less and less the most basic forms of communication with God.

A feeling of emptiness or lacking is usually a result of going through the motions. This feeling comes because we are trying to fill ourselves with things that cannot truly bring fulfillment. We try to find purpose in things that don't have purpose in and of themselves and look to our works to fulfill us rather than looking to Christ. This is one of the many reasons it's so important to spend time in prayer and in God's Word. Through these simple actions, God will show us that we have meaning in Him.

God wants to fill that area that feels lacking in your life. The more time you spend with Him, the more He will show you who He created you to be. The more time you spend in His Word, the more you will understand His calling for you. ***The actions and the motions themselves are not bad or wrong, but they become obstacles when we try to find fulfillment in them***. Only God can give us an abundant life. It's in knowing God that we find meaning and purpose in our actions. Otherwise, they become empty rituals.

Besides reading your Bible, praying, and seeking fulfillment in God, another action step you can take is to find an outlet through which to serve. Find something that you really enjoy doing– a gift or talent God has given you – and put it to use. I'm realizing more and more how important this is. God has given each of us unique talents and interests. What are those things that just come naturally to you? Consider what they are and how you can use them to honor God.

1 Peter 4:10-11 says this, "As each has received a gift, use it to serve one another, as good stewards of God's varied grace: whoever speaks, as one who speaks oracles of God; whoever serves, as one who serves by the strength that God supplies – in order that in everything God may be glorified through Jesus Christ. To him belong glory and dominion forever and ever. Amen."

You have been given a special gift by God, and He has called you to put it to use. This is not so that you can receive attention, but so that you might serve those around you and bring Him glory. Like I said in point number one, it's good that you've realized that you're on this unfulfilling path of going through the motions. That means that you have come to recognize that you are not giving God your all and that you have a desire to serve Him more. That's awesome! But now what are you going to do with that recognition?

Everyone has some way to serve others and bring glory to God. If you don't know what your gift is or if you feel like you don't have anything to give, pray about it. God is faithful and will show you how He wants to use you and will show you what you are gifted in. It doesn't matter what age you are; you are never too young to put your gifts to use and make a difference.

1 Timothy 4:12 says, "Don't let anyone look down on you because you are young, but set an example for the believers in speech, in conduct, in love, in faith and in purity."

We have been called, as young people, to set an example. God is able to use any age person, which includes you! You don't have to wait until after high school or after college or until you're able to travel to a different country on a mission trip, etc. God wants you to use what He's given you right where you are right – right now.

Getting off this path requires sacrifice, though. Refer to point number three.

The Bible tells us in Matthew 7:14 that "the gate is narrow and the way is hard that leads to life, and those who find it are few."

Walking on the path of life rather than the path of motions is tough. It's not super easy, it may not always be fun, and it is going to require sacrifice. But what is the reward for choosing this new path of sincere faith and this new lifestyle of truly seeking God? Life is the reward. And the best news is that God is not going to let you walk this path alone. He himself will be a lamp to your feet and a light to your path (Psalm 119:105). He will send other believers to strengthen you, and He calls you to also go out and be a source of strength for someone else. That's what living in community with other believers is all about.

Finding time to read your Bible every day, to pray, and to put your gifts to use is very difficult...trust me, I know! We live very busy lives that are constantly moving full speed ahead, and it's hard to keep up with life in general. God already warned us in his Word that it was not going to be easy, but He also promised life to those who walk with Him. Stop and think for a minute of the sacrifice God made for you. It's crazy! Jesus sacrificed *Himself* for you so that you could have life through Him. Now he's calling you to respond by making some small sacrifices in your life.

So yes, getting off the empty path of meaningless motions will require sacrifice, and it will come with trials and pain. But it also comes with the promise of life. It's up to you to count the cost. No one is forcing you onto any particular path and no one is holding you back. It's up to you whether or not you want to make that sacrifice. ***Do you want to keep going through the motions, or do you want to fully embrace the life God promises you?***

It's up to you whether or not you read your Bible, whether you spend time in prayer, and whether or not you use the gifts God has given you to serve others and glorify Him. I know it's hard, and I certainly do not practice these things perfectly. I'm not going to pretend or lie to you and say that sacrifice is easy, even if it's just simply a sacrifice of your time. I often struggle to choose to walk on the path of life. But I also have experienced the fact that when I do practice what God has called me to do and when I make that sacrifice of myself, true joy and fulfillment will follow. I hope and pray that you can have that experience too. That leads me to my last point.

God is always there. This is another one of those very basic concepts, yet it seems to be often forgotten. Even when it's really hard to keep going, even when it seems like there's no point in what you're doing, even when you feel like you can't get off the unfulfilling path of going through the motions, God is there. He never just disappears. He's there through it all, and He hears your heart's cry. He's there to help you.

All you have to do is ask. He's there to fill that lacking in your life, there to show you how you can serve Him, there in your pain and there in your rejoicing. He's there when you're on the path of motions and there when you walk fully in the life He's promised. Allow Him to be your source of strength because remember...there's absolutely no way you can truly know true joy and experience full life without Him.

Pray:

LORD, I pray that You would help me follow You down the narrow path.

You are my source of strength.

Holy Spirit, I ask that you empty me of me so that I can be filled with You.

Show me how You want to use me here.

I know I'm young, but I come to you with a willing heart.

I want to use my gifts to bring You glory.

I give You all that I am.

God, I don't want to just go through the motions. I don't want to feel empty.

I know that without You, I am nothing.

So God, take me and use me.

Form me into the person You want me to be.

And Jesus, I thank You for always being there for me, for never leaving my side.

Thank You for giving me a purpose and for the sacrifice You made for me.

I cannot thank You enough for the life You have given me.

Help me to use this life to bring You glory.

Amen.

I encourage you to stop right now and pray your own prayer. If you are struggling with getting off the path of meaningless motions and unfulfillment, pray that God will be your strength. If you don't feel like you're struggling with this, pray for someone who you know is dealing with this issue. Pray that God will continue to lead you and guide you.

Chapter 2: The Importance of Prioritizing

Who or what is first in your life?

Learn:

"Now as they went on their way, Jesus entered a village. And a woman named Martha welcomed him into her house. And she had a sister called Mary, who sat at the Lord's feet and listened to his teaching. But Martha was distracted with much serving. And she went up to him and said, 'Lord, do you not care that my sister has left me to serve alone? Tell her then to help me.' But the Lord answered her, 'Martha, Martha, you are anxious and troubled about many things, but one thing is necessary. Mary has chosen the good portion, which will not be taken away from her.'" *Luke 10:38-42*

To be completely honest with you, I have been struggling with the idea of prioritizing and truly setting Christ as the number one focus of my life. I'm still working on this quite a bit in my own life, but I've learned a lot through the process. I truly believe that in order to live a life with God as our number one priority, we have to surrender to Him and be humbled by Him every day because our flesh is constantly fighting against us.

When we lay everything else aside and truly make Christ the main focus and main priority, we are blessed! One of my favorite examples of this truth is in the story of Martha and Mary found in Luke 10. Every time I read this passage, I'm struck to the core because I realize that I am so often "a Martha" rather than "a Mary." One of the things that really interests me about this story is that Martha is the one who invites and welcomes Jesus into her home. Martha is the one who extends the invitation to Jesus in the first place, but then she becomes "distracted with much serving."

Often times, this is me. I have invited Jesus into my life – to come and be with me. But then I get distracted. And like Martha, I am usually distracted by things that are not "bad" in and of themselves. Martha was distracted by serving. Obviously, serving is not a bad thing; in fact, it's a great thing until it becomes a higher priority than God.

For me, some of my biggest distractions are school, grades, social media, family, and friends. Now, don't get me wrong, all of these things are great and important aspects of our everyday lives, but when I start setting them as higher priorities in my life than God, that's wrong and is just not healthy for my relationship with God. ***When I allow myself to become distracted by them, they then become obstacles that I've set in the way of me being able to simply sit at Jesus' feet.***

When we allow things to distract us, we become "anxious and troubled." Martha came to Jesus obviously very frustrated and annoyed with her sister for not helping. She came to Jesus for help or maybe for some sympathy, and His response was nothing short of amazing. His response also happens to hold the solution for Martha...and for us!

Jesus said, "you are anxious and troubled about many things, but one thing is necessary. Mary has chosen the good portion, which will not be taken away from her." Jesus doesn't condemn Martha for serving or tell her that serving is bad, but He is honest with her. He tells her that "...Only one thing is necessary. Mary has *chosen the good portion.*" And there is the key. Mary was able to see that Jesus was the good portion, and that being in His presence was all that was necessary. She *chose* to sit at Jesus' feet. She *chose* to partake in the thing that "would not be taken away from her." Mary had her priorities set straight while Martha did not. And as a result, Martha was anxious and troubled.

I know that life can get very hectic, but God commands us to "seek **first** the kingdom of God and his righteousness, and all these things will be added to you" (Matthew 6:33). Things like serving, school, family, sports, etc. are all good, but God wants us to seek Him before we seek those things. When we are seeking Him first, we are able to glorify Him in other areas of life and have peace that He will care for us in areas of need. (I encourage you to read Matthew 6:25-34. It talks all about how we should not be anxious about things here on earth, but instead should seek God first.)

When I was little, my mom used to remind me of this acronym for the word "joy," and I realize now how much it relates to setting priorities and avoiding anxiety. It went like this:

Jesus

Others

You

The point of this acronym was to show me that when I put Jesus first, others second, and me last, I would experience joy. I think that this is very true. When we have our priorities straight (Jesus, others, ourselves), we not only are obeying God by putting Him first and others above ourselves, but we will experience greater joy as a benefit.

This can be seen in the situation with Mary and Martha. Martha had her priorities a little mixed up and therefore wasn't experiencing joy, but rather she was anxious and troubled. God does not want for us to live this way; He wants for us to experience peace, joy, and fulfillment. He waits for us to take time to be still and quiet and really listen to what He's telling us. We also need to remember that God *deserves* to be first in our lives. ***Nothing else is worthy of being our utmost priority.*** Nothing else is worthy of our full attention or our praise. Christ sacrificed Himself for me, for you, for the world...it should be our desire to seek Him first and trust Him with everything else.

Act:

What are some actions we can take in order to make God our number one priority?

- Set goals for yourself.
- Set a goal for a certain amount of time you're going to spend reading your Bible every day.
  - All scripture is God breathed and useful for many things. It's also what will equip us to do the work God is calling us to. **(Read 2 Timothy 3:16-17)**
- Set goals in your prayer life. Set aside specific times to pray *and listen* to God.
  - It's God's will for us to be constant in prayer. We also have to remember that we are God's sheep, who need to listen and learn to know His voice. **(Read1 Thessalonians 5:16-18 and John 10:3-4)**
- Intentionally make time to sit at Jesus' feet, pushing aside all other distractions.
  - We should be like Mary, who made the choice to sit at Jesus' feet and spend time with Him rather than being distracted. **(Read Luke 10:39)**

- Have a friend keep you accountable.
  - Have someone you can trust ask you daily or maybe weekly if you are keeping God first in your life.
    - It's important to have someone who will help you up when you fall, someone who will be by your side and keep you accountable for your actions. **(Read Ecclesiastes 4:9-10)**
  - This will serve as a constant reminder to keep God first on a daily basis.
- Keep an eye on yourself.
  - You are going to know more than anyone whether or not you are truly seeking God first.
    - Examine yourself to see if you are walking in the ways of God. Are you following after God's character or after the character of the world? **(Read   2 Corinthians 13:5 and Romans 12:2)**
  - Continuously surrender yourself to God.
    - You must die to yourself in order to experience life with Christ. This world has nothing for us, and we can gain nothing from it. You must make the choice to surrender everything and follow Him. **(Read Matthew 16:24-27)**
  - Be mindful of how you use your time.

- Setting God as your number one priority also means you must use wisdom when deciding how you'll spend your time. Why wait for tomorrow to start spending your time wisely? **(Read Colossian 4:2, 5-6 and Ephesians 5:15-21)**
- It ultimately comes down to the daily choices you make and your motives behind them.
  - Do *everything* to bring God glory.**(Read 1 Corinthians 10:31)**
  - Chose to imitate the character of God on a day to day basis.**(Read Ephesians 5:1-2)**

*Be sure to look up these passages. They are there to encourage and guide you.

Pray:

Heavenly Father,

You are the only one I live for, and I seek you first.

I put aside all distractions, all things that make me anxious and troubled, and I look only to You.

My desire is to sit at Your feet and listen to You.

Help me to be like Mary, who chose the good portion.

I know that the things here on this earth will not last forever, but that Your love is eternal.

And I thank You for that.

God, I surrender all that I am to You right now.

I lay all that I am at Your feet.

Use me as You please.

Lord, you are my number one priority.

Help me to keep You first in *all* that I do.

You deserve and are worthy of all of my praise.

Amen.

Say your own prayer, surrendering all to Him. Tell God you want to make Him your number one priority. In the beginning of this chapter, I had listed a few things that were my "obstacles." Everyone has obstacles, whether they are people, hobbies, physical objects, etc. These essentially become the idols that we place in front of God. Think about your main obstacle(s) right now and lay them at the feet of Jesus. Allow Him to take control of every part of you and choose to seek Him first.

<u>Chapter 3: The Journey with Jesus</u>

Do you find yourself going through endless cycles of spiritual highs and lows?

Learn:

Have you ever gone to a retreat or on a missions trip with your church and by the end you feel like you're on a "spiritual high?" In other words, you feel like you're really on fire and really excited about God and what He's doing in your life and in the lives of those around you. Have you ever felt that way, but then gone home and within a week or so that fire and excitement seems to have disappeared? You're left confused and frustrated and just wanting to go back to that retreat because God seemed so present in your life while you were there. Well, if you can relate to this kind of experience, I'm right there with you. I know how this feels.

Here are four things that I've learned about spiritual highs:

1. It's natural to constantly want to be on a spiritual high because that's what we were created for.

2. We can't base our walks with Jesus on feelings.

3. As Christians, we need to understand that we are going to experience "highs," but that we will also face trials.

4. We need to remember that God has given us a mission to do.

Let me elaborate on each of these points...

1. It's natural to constantly want to be on a spiritual high because that's what we were created for.

I honestly think that it's natural for us to always want to be on that spiritual high because God has set eternity in our hearts (Ecclesiastes 3:11). We were created to always be in the presence of God, to walk with Him and to always be worshiping Him. However, when sin entered the world, we became separated from our Creator. Eternity has been set in our hearts, though; so we have a desire to constantly be with our God. We also have a sin nature, the flesh, which is constantly trying to suck us into following and worshiping the ways of the world. This world is fallen and broken, so there are going to be times when we get angry, frustrated, and confused.

The reality is that we will only experience the "ultimate" spiritual high (getting to be in the presence of God continuously without the brokenness of the world interrupting) when we get to heaven. However, we cannot forget the fact that, as Christians, Christ lives in us. This means that His presence is constantly in us.

The Holy Spirit lives in us and desires to work through us. If you do not constantly feel the power of His presence in your life that does not mean that His presence is not with you. That leads me to my second point.

2. We cannot base our walks with Jesus on feelings.

This point is a challenging one because so much of what we do and how we respond to situations is based off of feelings. I do believe that God's presence is meant to be *felt,* but we have to be cautious to not let *how we feel* determine our relationship with Jesus. For example, if you come out of a great time of corporate worship "feeling good," but wake up the next morning and no longer have that feeling, you cannot than determine that because you don't feel the way you did the day before that God's Spirit is no longer with you. You must recognize the fact that during the time of corporate worship, you **experienced the presence of God in a deeper and more intimate way.** But you also must recognize that **that same Spirit which you experienced so intimately rules and reigns inside of you every day.** We have full access to the presence of God at all times because He lives in us! God is the same yesterday, today, and forever...even when our feelings change.

3. As Christians, we need to understand that we are going to experience trials.

There is no doubt that this world is broken and that we all face different trials every day. There are going to be times in our Christian walk when we feel very alive and excited spiritually, and there are going to be times that are hard.

According to Ecclesiastes 3:1-8, "There is a season, and a time for every matter under heaven: a time to be born, and a time to die; a time to plant, and a time to pluck up what is planted; a time to kill, and a time to heal; a time to break down, and a time to build up; a time to weep, and a time to laugh; a time to mourn, and a time to dance; a time to cast away stones, and a time to gather stones together; a time to embrace, and a time to refrain from embracing; a time to seek, and a time to lose; a time to keep, and time to cast away; a time to tear, and a time to sew; a time to keep silence, and a time to speak; a time to love and a time to hate; a time for war and a time for peace."

Not only are there going to be things like laughing, dancing, embracing, weeping, mourning, and loss, but there is actually an appropriate and appointed time for each of them. This fact is not an excuse to give up, to get mad, or to push God to the side for a while until things get better. In the highs, the lows, and everywhere in between, it's extremely important to remember that God is our strength; we cannot rely on our own strength. God is faithful and will never leave you in the midst of a trial.

It's also important to realize that we do not always understand why certain things happen when they do or the way they do, and it's okay that we don't.

The Bible says to "trust in the LORD with all your heart, and do not lean on your own understanding. In all your ways acknowledge him, and he will make straight your paths" (Proverbs 3:5).

It doesn't tell us to trust partly in ourselves and partly in God, but rather to trust Him with all of our hearts. That means in the highs of our life, we are to trust Him and lean on Him completely. In the trials, we are to trust Him and lean on Him completely. And everywhere in between the highs and lows, we are to trust Him and lean on Him completely.

Another key to remember in the highs, lows, and in-betweens is that God is using your different situations to strengthen and shape you. It can be easy to see and rejoice about how God is strengthening and shaping you in the highs of your life, but it can be very difficult to say the same during the trials.

James tells us that we should "count it all joy, my brothers, when you meet trials of various kinds, for you know that the testing of your faith produces steadfastness. And let steadfastness have its full effect, that you may be perfect and complete, lacking in nothing" (James 1:2-4).

So it's important to remember that in the end, the trials and low points are going to strengthen and perfect you. We are commanded to seek joy through the trials, knowing that although we have to walk through them, we are not defeated by them; in fact, we are already victorious through them. Jesus has overcome the world - He's already won the victory for us (John 16:33)! So, whenever you go through a trial, seek joy and keep a victorious mindset.

4. We need to remember that God has given us a mission to do.

It's not at all a bad thing to go on a missions trip or retreat and experience a spiritual high. It's never bad to get excited for Christ. When returning from a missions trip or retreat, however, we need to remember that our mission continues.

This does not necessarily mean it will always be easy, or even super fun. It simply means that your mission continues; that it does not end when the missions trip or retreat ends. What is our mission? ***Our mission is to love God and love others with all that we are***. We are to make disciples out of all the nations, acting justly and walking humbly with God (Matthew 28:19, Mark 12:29-31, Micah 6:8). And this mission continues for as long as we are here on earth.

Act:

After you get back from a retreat or missions trip, what are some actions you can take to remain focused on your mission? What should you do after a spiritual high? How do you keep from "crashing" afterwards? I'm going to go through some basic steps that I find helpful when trying to answer these questions.

- When you get back, set practical goals for yourself - not unrealistic ones.

- Set practical goals that will work for you and your schedule. If you aren't currently doing devotions/spending time with God daily, start doing that. Find a time that you know will work for you and find a place where you know you won't be distracted. If you are already consistently spending quiet time with God, maybe you could add to it. You could also consider finding practical ways in your church, community, or school to serve.

- Remember that you are capable of nothing on your own.

  - Oftentimes when I come off of a spiritual high, I start thinking of different things *I* can do. How *I* can change things. How *I* am going to have such a big impact on people. Then I have to stop in my tracks and say, "No, I can do nothing on my own. God, please work in me and through me because *You* are the only one who can change a person's heart."

John 15:5 says this, "I am the vine; you are the branches. Whoever abides in me and I in him, he it is that bears much fruit, for apart from me you can do nothing."

So, when you come off a spiritual high, remember that God abides in you and you in Him. Don't think that you can change anything, because you can't. Rather, have a willing and open heart and allow God to use you.

- Trials will eventually come….so let God use them to strengthen you.
  - This point is pretty straightforward. Trials are inevitable in this life. But, trials are meant to strengthen us and shape us into more mature Christians. Pray through these trials. Seek joy through them and remember that God has already won the victory for you. Ask God what He's trying to teach you and submit to Him. Sometimes the lesson is as simple as a reminder of our own weakness and need for God.
- Allow your experiences to fill you up.

- When you are able to benefit from the experiences of retreats, missions trips, or other types of "getaways," take advantage of the opportunity to spend one-on-one time with God. Take advantage of the fact that there is an environment being created that is free of all of the usual distractions. You're away from home and you have the time and space to really focus on your relationship with God. Allow these times to fill you and refresh you. Then, when you go home, take the things you learned during those times and apply them.
- Don't forget about your mission!
  - When coming off a spiritual high, it's easy to get wrapped up in what happened or in the fact that you now have to face "reality." Life can be crazy, and when we come home from a "mountaintop experience," it's so easy to get swept up again in the ways of the world. But remember the mission God has given you! We all have a purpose here on this earth. As a teenager, it can be very easy to make excuses. **You may have heard people tell you that your only job right now is to get through school or that God's plan for your life will "really" start when you get to college, but neither of those**

statements are true. We are called to live for God *every day* by honoring Him and loving those around us like Christ loves us. Keep your focus on God and pursue Him with all that you are.

Pray:

Lord,

Thank you for allowing me to experience You in intimate ways.

Thank You for the trials and how You use them to strengthen my faith.

I pray that in both the highs and lows, You would teach me and strengthen me.

I know that I am capable of nothing without You.

So God, I give myself to You.

Let your light shine through me so those around me would see You.

Teach me to love like You love and serve like You serve.

I want to follow You all the days of my life.

My desire is to bring You praise.

Amen.

I encourage you to pray and thank God for whatever place He has you in your life right now. Ask Him to teach you and guide you through it. Tell Him that you are willing to follow Him and to take on the mission He's set before you.

<u>Chapter 4: Obligation vs. Desire</u>

Is spending time with God a duty or a joy?

Learn:

If I were to ask you *why* you spend time with God (I'm referring to time specifically set aside to be in His word, to pray, and to listen to Him), how would you respond? I'm going to spend this chapter talking about why we spend time with God and why our mindset about spending time with Him is so important.

Obligation:

Spending time with God should not be an obligation in the same way that spending time with a best friend should never feel like an obligation. It's not a healthy mindset if the only reason you're taking time to pray and read the Bible is because you feel like you have to, or that otherwise you won't be a "good" Christian, or because you need to cross it off your list of things to do. Also, if God has become someone who is just an obligation for you in your life, that is most likely a sign that He is not your number one priority. If you enter into spending time with God with the mindset of obligation, you most likely will not be very focused and will probably not get much out of that time.

I can say all this because I've been through this. Honestly, when I think of spending time with God as something that is simply obligatory, I catch myself not caring much whether or not I get something out of the time. *I become more concerned with the fact that I spent time reading the Bible (check that off the list!) than I am about what God is actually trying to show me through what I read*. This is not a good way to think about your relationship with God.

Now, don't get me wrong, sometimes taking time out of a busy day to spend with God is a hard discipline. Especially in the beginning, it is very much like building a habit. But the more you do it, the more it will no longer be a habit, but it will come out of genuine desire and joy. And desire is the opposite of obligation...we'll talk about that later.

Another symptom of an obligatory relationship with God is that you become blinded. You become blinded to the reality that spending time with God is *not* a once a day or once a week activity that you can simply "do" and then be done with. God is always with you. As basic as that sounds, it's a reality that is often forgotten, especially when a relationship with God becomes obligatory. However, the fact that God is always with you does not then mean that you should neglect taking time to be alone with Him. He still wants our undivided attention, and we will always need that dedicated, quiet time with Him.

Desire/Need:

When we think about spending time with God, we should view it not as an obligation, but rather as a desire. We should seek after God and long to be with Him.

King David put it this way in Psalm 63:1:"O God, you are my God; earnestly I seek you; my soul thirsts for you; my flesh faints for you, as in a dry and weary land where there is no water."

Your desire for quiet time with God should be driven by your awareness of your need for Him.

Jesus made our need for Him very clear in John 14:6 when He said, "I am the way, and the truth, and the life. No one comes to the Father except through me."

Jesus is the only way. He is our only hope. We desperately need Him.

The Bible tells us that "all have sinned and fall short of the glory of God" but it also says that when you accept Christ as your Lord and Savior that "by grace you have been saved through faith. And this is not your own doing; it is the gift of God, not a result of works, so that no one may boast" (Romans 3:23 and Ephesians 2:8-9).

Salvation is a gift from God; there are no actions that will ever be able to earn salvation. If we believe Scripture, then we believe that we have all fallen short of God's glory. Yet He chose to offer us salvation as a gift because there is no possible way for us to earn it. If this is not the definition of having a desperate need for God, then I don't know what is! When you realize the price Jesus paid for you and that without him, you'll never experience abundant life, your heart's response should be to lay everything at His feet. You should have a *desire* to spend time with Him and a desire to get to know His character more.

If you go into spending time with God with a mindset of desire and need for God, you most likely will not be very distracted and you will get a lot out of your time. I say this because I have experienced this. When I have the mindset of desiring God rather than feeling like time with God is an obligation, I find that my heart is much more open and willing to hear what He has for me.

And as I continue to learn more about who God is, I realize more and more just how much I need Him. I realize more and more that without Him I am nothing, and that increases my desire for Him. Do you see how this can become a perpetual cycle of growth in your love for God? And it all starts by simply recognizing the reality of our deep need.

Look back again at what Psalm 63:1 says. David says that his soul thirsts for God and his flesh faints for Him. This is clearly a description of David's longing and desire for God. David goes on to say that his soul and flesh desire God "as in a dry and weary land where there is no water." A dry and weary land is in *need* of water. Because of its need for water, it also *desires* water. This is exactly how our relationship with God looks. We are dry and weary, and so we need and desire God – the source of life giving water – to come rain on us.

When you realize your need for God, you will then have a greater desire for Him. As your desire for Him increases and you spend more time with Him, you gain a better understanding of who God is and all He's done for you, which leads to you realize even more so how great your need for Him is. And so the cycle continues, and as it continues you grow in God and discover more and more about who He is and who He made you to be. The feeling of obligation disappears because you will so strongly desire Him and because you will realize that without Him you are just a dry, weary land in desperate need of water.

There is one thing that I want to make sure that I clarify. If you are stuck in the mindset of God being an obligation to you rather than a desire, that does not mean that God is angry with you. It also does not mean that you should give up on trying to set aside time to spend with Him because He can and will still use those times. He will honor your commitment to Him by blessing you with greater desire. Just pray for it, and He will give you the right perspective.

Act:

What are some actions you can take to set God as a desire in your life?

- Remind yourself of your need for Him.
  - Remind yourself on a daily basis of all that God's done for you. Continuously remind yourself about how much you need Him and thank Him for fulfilling all of your needs. Look up some Scriptures about how you need God. As your understanding of your need for Him grows, so will your desire to be with Him. **(Read Romans 5:6-11 and John 3:16-18)**
- It's okay to start small and to not focus only on what is quantitative.
  - What I mean is that you don't have to read multiple chapters of your Bible each day or spend a certain amount of time everyday in quiet time with God. God cares more about your heart, and He wants for you to get to know Him better. *It's not about whether or not you accomplished a large amount of reading in your Bible. It's about whether you're growing in your*

relationship with God **(Read 1 Peter 2:2).** It's about quality over quantity. For example, I encouraged you to go through this devotional slowly, not just because the chapters are long and can be broken up into multiple days, but because it's actually good for us to slow down sometimes – to think, pray, and listen more instead of simply doing more.

- Don't turn the feeling of obligation into an excuse to not spend time with God.
  - Like I talked about in the previous chapter, we're all going to have highs and lows in our walks with God. If you're feeling like God has become an obligation, that is an even better reason to really spend some focused time with Him. **(Read Jeremiah 29:13)**
- God promised to be there to open the door - all you have to do is knock.
  - If you have accepted Christ as your Lord and Savior, you are now a child of God. God loves you, cares for you, and desires you. God is constant in His love for you, and He wants you to seek after Him. When you do seek after Him, He promises to be there. So whether you feel like God is an obligation right now or whether you desire Him with all of your heart, know that when you knock on His door, He'll be right there to open it.

You have to make the choice, though. You have to choose to seek after Him. **(Read Romans 8:14-17 and Luke 11:9-13)**

Pray:

Lord, You are the desire of my heart.

I can't even comprehend all that You've done for me.

I need You more than anything else on this earth.

I want to get to know You more.

I want to understand You more.

God, speak to me and teach me.

Teach me more about who I am in You.

I know that You've promised that when I seek You, I will find You.

So God, I seek you with all of my heart.

I chase after You.

Even when it's hard, I'll chase after You

because I know You will guide me through it.

Thank You for loving me and for making me Your child.

Thank You for Your sacrifice and for constantly loving me,

even when I turn away from You.

Lord, I love You, and I give You all of my praise.

Amen.

I encourage you to take a minute or two right now to thank God for everything He's done for you. Take time to tell God that you need Him and that you want Him. Ask yourself if you feel like it's an obligation or a desire to spend time with God. No matter what situation you're in right now, ask Him to guide you through life, to go before you and to be the light to your feet.

<u>Chapter 5: Health and Fitness</u>

Have you been exercising your mind, heart, and soul to be more like Christ?

Learn:

We all know that physical exercise is very important and beneficial to us. Getting in good shape physically requires a lot of dedication. Not only is it important to exercise, but we also must make wise choices about what we eat. When we do dedicate ourselves to exercising regularly as well as fueling our bodies with healthy, nutritious foods, our discipline pays off. We start to see results as we continuously strive to be more physically fit.

Now, I'm not telling you these things because I want to give you a mini health lesson but rather because I want to relate these concepts to our spiritual lives. Just like it's important *and* beneficial to stay fit physically, it's also important and beneficial to stay fit spiritually. There are two main things that you need to do in order to stay fit spiritually.

#1 – Exercise regularly

#2 – Fuel yourself properly

When you act upon these two concepts you'll begin to grow and change and really see results. Let me explain in more detail.

Exercising

Exercising your mind, heart, and soul is one of the key elements to living a life that is spiritually fit. What do I mean by exercising your mind, heart, and soul? I mean that you should train and devote your whole self to being committed to Christ. Healthy Christians should always be striving to become more like Christ.

1 John 2:6 says this: "Whoever says he abides in him ought to walk in the same way in which he walked."

The goal you're trying to reach in exercising is to live the way Jesus lived. Obviously, living the exact lifestyle of Jesus is impossible because we are all sinful and Jesus lived a perfect life. This fact should not discourage you, but rather motivate you to keep exercising. Jesus lived a perfect life and suffered the harsh penalty for all of our sins so that we might have life through Him. Training our minds, hearts, and souls to respond to situations the way Christ would respond is a great step toward becoming spiritually fit.

Another great exercise for your mind, heart, and soul is simply to love God and to learn to love Him more every day.

In Matthew 22:37 Jesus says, "You shall love the Lord your God with all your heart and with all your soul and with all your mind."

This is a great exercise that you can put to practice every day. Loving God isn't always easy, but it's of the utmost importance. Read the verse again very carefully. There's a word that keeps appearing throughout this short statement. The word is *all.* This is a key word; without it, our exercise would look very different. God does not call us to love Him with "part of" or "some of" or even "most of" our heart, soul, and mind. He also doesn't say to love Him only in the good times or only when we desperately need His help. ***God has called us to love Him with all that we are and in every aspect of our lives.*** The thing is, we are fallen people and we struggle to love God with all that we are. Now this is where the exercising comes in. We need to be training our whole selves to continuously love God.

If you're practicing the first exercise (training yourself to live like Christ), you will find that your love for Him will deepen. And as your love for Him deepens, you will also find that this last exercise I'm going to share with you will become easier and easier.

The last exercise in becoming spiritually fit is to serve others. This idea is actually directly related to the first exercise because Jesus lived a life of service to others.

In Philippians 2:4-8 Paul says, "Let each of you look not only to his own interests, but also to the interests of others. Have this mind among yourselves, which is yours in Christ Jesus, who though he was in the form of God, did not count equality with God a thing to be grasped, but emptied himself, by taking the form of a servant, being born in the likeness of men. And being found in human form, he humbled himself by becoming obedient to the point of death, even death on a cross."

Look at the very first sentence in that set of verses. Looking to the "interests of others" is such an incredible exercise. Laying aside your own desires in order to joyfully serve another person requires your whole self to be humbled! The verses that follow set in place for us the greatest demonstration of someone (Christ) who humbled Himself in order to serve others.

We should not only strive to serve others the way Christ served, but we should also be motivated by His act of humility and service to us. These exercises are going to require a lot of dedication. If you stay disciplined with them, you will be stretched and pushed. And like any exercise that you commit to and that you let stretch you a little bit, you will see great results. As you train your whole self to become more spiritually fit, you will notice yourself changing. *You will be transformed from the inside out because that's what God does – He transforms your life as you pursue Him.*

Fueling Yourself

In order to become spiritually fit, it's also import to be fueling yourself in a beneficial way. I'm not referring to eating healthy. I'm referring to what you surround yourself with on a daily basis. What types of things are you listening to, watching, and partaking in? Are they things that are going to properly fuel you to take on God's mission for your life? We are constantly surrounded by all types of social media, movies, music, etc. that are sending us a variety of messages. Now, I'm not saying that all secular music is bad, that we should never partake in social media, or that we have to watch only G rated movies. What I *am* saying is that it's very important to guard yourself.

Proverbs 4:23 says this: "Above all else, guard your heart, for everything you do flows from it."

The things you "consume" on a daily basis will eventually be visible through your words and actions. *In becoming spiritually fit, it's key to fuel yourself with things that are going to build you up in order to better serve and glorify God.* What you take in will be evident in what you give out. You should be mindful of how you're fueling yourself because it will come out in all that you do and because you're the temple of God.

In 1 Corinthians 3:16-17 Paul says, "Do you not know that you are God's temple and that God's Spirit dwells in you? ...God's temple is holy, and you are that temple."

Later in 1 Corinthians 6:19-20 Paul says, "Or do you not know that your body is a temple of the Holy Spirit within you, whom you have from God? You are not your own, for you were bought with a price. So glorify God in your body."

God has bought you at a price and now dwells within you. You yourself are the temple of God and so you must be mindful of the things you are allowing to enter God's temple. As Christians, we are not supposed to fuel our lives with things of the world. **Paul puts it this way in Romans 12:2: "Do not be conformed to this world, but be transformed by the renewal of your mind, that by testing you may discern what is the will of God, what is good and acceptable and perfect."**

We should not be fueled by what the world has to offer, but rather, we are called to be fueled by God's transforming work in our lives. As we are fueled by God's Word and His presence, we will then be further motivated to share that amazing transformative power with others. The bottom line: ***This world is incapable of properly fueling you to complete the mission God has for you.*** Look to God to fuel your life!

So then what should we do with things like social media and music? Even things like sports, family, and friends – what do we do with what the world has to offer us? Many of these things are actually good and they can be beneficial. However, they can so easily be disguised as things that will fuel our lives and we often make idols out of them and end up depending on them to fulfill and energize us.

It's okay to allow these things to bless and benefit your life, but the real question is whether or not God is pleased in the way you make use of these things. This is where the guarding comes in. Are the things you read and look at on social media pleasing to God? Do the lyrics of the music you listen to honor God? These are the kinds of questions we really have to ask and answer honestly if we want to evaluate how we are fueling our lives.

If you answered no to those questions above, then you are in an awesome place to allow God to transform you! You may need to reevaluate how much you're guarding what you are putting into the temple of God. Remember that ultimately God is your fuel for life, but that you also need to be careful about everything you take in on a daily basis. The goal is to become spiritually fit, and this takes discipline.

Act:

It can be hard to start exercising and fueling yourself correctly, especially when there are so many distractions. Here is some encouragement that will hopefully motivate you to take the next step in your spiritual fitness.

1. Ask for God's strength daily.

    - Spiritual health and fitness can be tough with the many distractions around us. But remind yourself that "**[you] can do all things through him who strengthens [you]**" **(Philippians 4:13).**

    - If you are pushing yourself to become more like Christ, to love and serve those around you, and to guard yourself from the ways of the world, that's awesome! It's even more awesome that we serve a God who provides us with the strength to accomplish these things.

2. Don't focus on only exercise or only the fuel you need.

    - When you both exercise and fuel yourself properly, you are making yourself as ready as possible to be used by God. If you only exercise your spiritual life, you'll quickly become drained...especially if you're fueling yourself with things of the world. But if you're only fueling yourself and don't put anything into practice, you won't bear any fruit. So be sure to remember that exercising and fueling go hand in hand.

3. Step out in greater exercise as you learn to be fueled by Him.

- The more you exercise, the more you'll need to be fueled. The more you are fueled, the more you'll want to exercise. There will be some bumps along the road where this cycle will not seem so easy. But remember that **God** is your strength and He will never leave your side!

4. Never give up. Make health and fitness a daily focus.

- Your training here on Earth is never finished. Exercising your mind, heart, and soul and fueling yourself properly are not one-time experiences. They are both disciplines that should be constantly lived out on a daily basis.

- The Bible tells us that we should **"...lay aside every weight and sin which clings so closely, and let us run with endurance the race that is set before us, looking to Jesus, the founder and perfecter of our faith..." (Hebrews 12:1-2).** You should never give up; never stop running your race. As you work to become more spiritually fit, remember to look to Jesus and to just keep running.

Pray:

Father, I ask that You would be my strength as I strive to know You and honor You.

Thank You that You are there to help, motivate, and challenge me.

Jesus, I want to be more like You.

I want to serve how You serve and love like You love.

I'm sorry for trying to fuel myself with things that don't please You.

You are all that truly fuels me, Lord.

You are the one who puts breath in my lungs.

And so I give You all the praise.

I want to become more spiritually fit so I can do what you've called me to do.

I know that it will be challenging at times, but I also know You are there to help me.

Thank You for buying me back and for transforming my life.

Help me to share what You've done in my life with others.

Continue to transform and mold me into who You want me to be.

God, I love You with all of my heart, soul, and mind.

Amen.

Take a minute to pray your own prayer to God. Ask Him to continuously transform your life. If there are things in your life that you know you should not be taking in, ask God to give you the strength to give up the empty, unfulfilling fuel of this world. Confess to Him, and He will forgive you. ***Rest assured that He will be the only fuel you'll ever need***.

<u>Chapter 6: Worship – Anytime, Anyplace</u>

Are you living a lifestyle of worship?

Learn:

Christians often view worship as a group of people coming together, playing instruments, and singing songs to God. This indeed *is* worship, but worship is not limited to this. There are many expressions of worship, and singing to God is just one of them. So, what exactly is involved in worshiping God? Worship is praising, glorifying and lifting up Jesus because he deserves it. It's something that flows out of you from your love and reverence for Him. Worship also goes far beyond singing a few songs once a week at church. It's something that becomes a way of life; something that becomes a natural part of every action. **Worship is a lifestyle choice.** In fact, choosing to live a lifestyle of worship means leading a sacrificial life.

In Romans 12:1 Paul says, "...present your bodies as a living sacrifice, holy and acceptable to God, which is your spiritual worship."

What Paul is saying in the verse above is that we should offer our whole selves to be used by God, as an act of worship. Worship is giving back to God, and Paul is reminding us that when we give back, we should give it *all.*

Act:

Throughout my walk with Christ I have come to find many things to be true about this idea of living a *lifestyle* of worship. I want to share some of what I've learned with you.

1. Living a lifestyle of worship is a daily decision.
2. The more you learn about who God is the more you'll understand what it looks like to live a lifestyle of worship.
3. Worship is not confined to a certain place or time.
4. It's a great way to allow God's light to shine through you.
5. God is truly the only one who deserves to be worshiped.

Let's go through each one of these concepts, break them apart, and look at them a little deeper.

1. Living a lifestyle of worship is a daily decision.

For worship to truly become a lifestyle, it has to be a choice you make every day. That means that even on the days when it's hard to worship, we have the ability to choose worship. ***Every day we are faced with the decision to either give back to God or to hold back from God.*** In giving back to God, we are acting in a manner of worship, but when we hold back from God we act out of selfishness and, ultimately, out of a lack of trust. God does not force us to worship Him; He doesn't force us to give anything back. He allows us to make those decisions because He's given us a free will.

Every morning when you wake up, say to God "Today I choose to worship You. I want to give everything back to You, and I want to bring you glory though all of my actions." Make this a daily commitment. Teach your heart to worship in both the good and bad times.

2. The more we learn about who God is the more we begin to understand what it looks like to live a lifestyle of worship.

When you take time to study the character of God, the idea of a worship lifestyle will become a much clearer concept. Why is this so? Because when we understand more about *who* God is, we also gain a better understanding of who we are and *why* we should worship Him. It would be foolish to worship someone you knew absolutely nothing about.

In Psalm 95:1-6 the psalmist says, "Oh come, let us sing to the LORD; let us make a joyful noise to the rock of our salvation! Let us come into his presence with thanksgiving… For the LORD is a great God, and a great King above all gods. In his hand are the depths of the earth; the heights of the mountains are his also. The sea is his, for he made it, and his hands formed the dry land.

Oh come, let us worship and bow down; let us kneel before the LORD, our Maker!"

It's obvious that this psalmist knew God and was eager to worship Him because of what he knew. He recognizes God as "the rock of our salvation," the "King above all gods," and the "Maker." The psalmist also points out how God displays His greatness through His control over creation. The author had taken time to get to know God as his Rock, King, and Maker and out of this understanding came the overflow of a lifestyle of worship.

3. Worship is not confined to a certain place or time.

This is one of the most important concepts to understand when it comes to living out a lifestyle of worship. Sunday morning at church is a great place to worship, but it goes so much farther than that! *Living a lifestyle of worship is all about how you live in between Sunday mornings.* Worship is meant for anytime and anyplace.

This means when we're at school, work, or with our sports teams, our main focus should be to worship God. It might look a little different in each situation, but the main goal is to be a "living sacrifice" by bringing glory to God.

This also means that when you're by yourself, you still live to glorify and honor God. Living a true lifestyle of worship means that when it's just you and God - with no one else around - you will not cease to worship Him. Even when we may feel tired or just want to give up, our hearts should still desire to worship Him.

4. It's a great way to allow God's light to shine through you.

I've often been reminded of the concept that my own life is my most effective witnessing tool. We are constantly surrounded by people, many of whom are lost because they don't follow Christ. Our responses (even to the littlest things) are being observed by the people around us. If we are seeking to live a lifestyle of worship, people will notice. Why will they notice? Well, remember, we said that worship is sacrificial. And isn't sacrifice the very opposite of the selfish ways of the world? So by living a lifestyle of worship, we are able to be a light to the world. A life sold out to Christ is the very best witness of all.

In Matthew 5:14-16 Jesus says, "You are the light of the world. A city set on a hill cannot be hidden. Nor do people light a lamp and put it under a basket, but on a stand, and it gives light to all in the house. In the same way, let your light shine before others, so that they may see your good works and give glory to your Father who is in heaven."

God has chosen YOU to be the light in this dark world. You were not meant to be hidden or covered up, but to be exposed so that Christ's light can shine through you brightly. One of the best ways to "let your light shine before others" is to live your life as a sacrifice of worship to God. As you daily choose to live a life of worship, you will "give glory to your Father who is in heaven."

5. God is truly the only one who deserves to be worshiped.

Just like it would be foolish to worship someone who you knew absolutely nothing about, it would also be foolish to worship someone who did not deserve to be worshiped. *The only one who is worthy of worship is God. No one else even comes close.*

Yet we often hold back our worship from God. We refuse to live that sacrificial lifestyle of worship. Sometimes we even give our worship to things that don't deserve it. It's when we remember the greatness of God that we realize how foolish we are for trying to worship the created rather than the Creator. **In Psalm 145:3 David says, "Great is the LORD and most worthy of praise; his greatness no one can fathom."**

God is so incredible that we cannot even comprehend just how amazing He is! Because He is so unfathomable, our response should be to worship Him and lay our lives down as a living sacrifice to Him. Think about it this way: nothing can compare to God because no one else was able to sacrifice themselves in order to save you. Only Jesus could have accomplished that...and He did! His greatness is more than we can even wrap our minds around. But one thing we know for sure is that God truly is the only one who deserves to be worshiped.

Pray:

Father, my desire is to live a lifestyle of worship.

I want to live a sacrificial life for You so that I can bring You all the glory.

You're the only one who deserves worship.

Help me to be a light for You through the way I live my life.

Teach me what it really looks like to worship any time and any place.

I want to worship You every day of my life.

You're all that I need.

I can't even begin to understand how great You are.

And so I will worship You.

I make the choice right now to worship You.

I choose to give myself over to You.

You are worthy of all of my worship.

I love You Lord.

Amen.

Take a minute right now to make that choice to give all your worship to Him. Just think about His greatness and how worthy He is of your worship. Allow God to shine through you as you choose to live a sacrificial life. Ask God to teach you daily what it means to live a lifestyle of worship.

<u>Chapter 7: Hearing God's Voice</u>

Do you ever feel like God is so distant that you can't hear His voice?

Learn:

"Then the LORD called Samuel, and he said, 'Here I am!' and ran to Eli and said, 'Here I am, for you called me.' But he said, 'I did not call; lie down again.' So he went and lay down. And the lord called again, 'Samuel!' and Samuel arose and went to Eli and said, 'Here I am, for you called me.' But he said, 'I did not call, my son; lie down again.' Now Samuel did not yet know the LORD, and the word of the LORD had not yet been revealed to him. And the LORD called Samuel again the third time. And he arose and went to Eli and said, 'Here I am, for you called me.' Then Eli perceived that the LORD was calling the boy. Therefore Eli said to Samuel, 'Go, lie down, and if he calls you, you shall say, 'Speak, LORD, for your servant hears.' So Samuel went and lay down in his place. *(1 Samuel 3:4-9)*

I had always thought that God calling Samuel's name in the night was such a cool story. I was always interested in the fact that God spoke audibly to Samuel and thought it was kind of funny that Samuel didn't realize that it was God. But there is one statement in this passage that I had never picked up on before...not until this past year, that is.

I was on a weekend retreat with one of my older sisters when this passage in 1 Samuel was brought to my attention by God. I was actually on the retreat to help my sister lead worship for the different sessions. At the end of one of the sessions, the youth pastor got up and said that at that time, we were going to do what they called "the hour." The hour was simply a block of 60 minutes, during which everyone went out into the woods and found a spot where they would be completely alone. This was meant to be a time of prayer, reflection, and listening – just me and God.

And so I went out into the woods and as I was praying, I began to question God. I was asking Him things like "why do you feel so far from me?" and "why can't I hear your voice?" and "how do I know when it's your voice?" This is when I started reading about the boy who audibly heard God call his name in the night. As I was reading 1 Samuel 3, there was one verse that jumped out at me and as I read it over and over. I started to realize why I was battling to hear God. **The verse that caught my attention was verse 7, which states this: "Now Samuel did not yet know the LORD, and the word of the LORD had not yet been revealed to him."**

This may seem like an odd verse, but let me share with you why it hit me so hard. This verse is the reason given for *why* Samuel kept running to Eli when he didn't understand that it was God calling his name. There are two reasons Samuel didn't "hear" God's voice.

1) Samuel didn't <u>know God.</u>
2) Samuel didn't know <u>the word of God.</u>

Samuel didn't know God in the sense that he was not involved in a personal relationship with God. Also, Samuel had not been exposed to the Scriptures. When I read 1 Samuel 3:7, I understood right away that there was a reason why I felt so distant from God and why I wasn't hearing or clearly knowing if God was speaking to me. In fact, there were two reasons.

1) I was not taking time to get to know God.
2) I was not spending any time in <u>the word of God.</u>

Sitting there alone in the woods, I remembered that God desires to have an intimate friendship with his children. God does not call us his acquaintances; rather he calls us his friends. (See **John 15:15**) The more time you spend with a friend, the more you'll get to know their voice. You get so familiar with their voice that you don't even have to see them in order to know that it's them. In the same way, ***the more time you spend with God the more you'll recognize His voice.***

Act:

Let me go back to those three main questions that I had been asking God before He brought my attention to 1 Samuel, chapter 3. I want to share with you what God has taught me about those questions.

1. Why does God feel so far from me?

- *Do you feel like you just want God to be near to you?*
James tells us this, "Draw near to God, and he will draw near to you." (James 4:8)

If you're feeling like God is distant from you, the absolute best thing to do is to draw near to God. One thing that I have learned to be very true is that God does not distance Himself from us. He is always with us and will never leave our side. If there is distance between you and God, it's important to know first and foremost that God did not create that distance.

Picture Jesus standing across from you. He's very close to you. Now, imagine setting large blocks between you and Jesus. The more blocks you set down, the more distance is created between the two of you. The blocks represent anything that is keeping you from being near to Him; maybe it's something, someone, or maybe it's a sin that you haven't surrendered to Him. In order for you to be capable of drawing near to God, you must surrender anything that is creating distance between you and your Savior. The blocks have to be removed.

Also, be encouraged in the fact that you're not the only one who has ever felt far from God. This concept is not new to the human race. In fact, David too felt this way.

In Psalm 13:1, 5-6 David says, "How long, O LORD? Will you forget me forever? How long will you hide your face from me? ...But I have trusted in your steadfast love; my heart shall rejoice in your salvation. I will sing to the LORD, because he has dealt bountifully with me."

David starts off the Psalm questioning God, asking Him why He's so distant from him. But David ends the Psalm by reminding himself of God's constant love toward him. He ends by singing to God, by drawing near to God. David says that he has "trusted in [God's] steadfast love." ***When you feel far from God, will you choose to trust in His steadfast love?*** Will you trust His promises and will you pray and sing to Him even though you feel distant?

So, if you are asking God why He's so far from you, remember to:

- Draw near to Him
- Surrender anything that is creating distance between you and Him
- Trust God because His love has never failed you before

- Know that when you seek Him, He'll draw near to you

2. Why can't I hear His voice?

- *Are you wondering how to build a habit of listening to God?*

I already touched on this a little bit in the "Learn" section, but I want to go deeper into this topic. The two points I had made before, that were based off of 1 Samuel 3:7, were that you need to take time to get to know God and you need to spend time in His Word. A third point to add is that if you want to hear His voice, you must listen for His voice. These were the three basic concepts that helped me to understand why I couldn't hear God's voice. Now the question becomes, "how do I go about putting these concepts into practice?"

Knowing God:

Think of someone who's really close to you, who you know very well. Now ask yourself, "How did I get to know that person so well?" Your answer is probably something to the effect of "because I've spent a lot of time with that person" or "because we talk to each other all the time" or maybe "because I've grown up with that person.*" In order to know God, you must also spend time with Him, talk with Him, and grow with Him.*

Here are some practical ways that you can get to know God more:

- Get involved with a church and/or youth group if you're not already

- Spend time in prayer daily (chat with God like you would chat with a friend)

- Spend time in God's Word (try committing some of your favorite verses to memory)

Everyone is going to hear God's voice in different ways, which is really awesome. That's because ***God knows you so intimately that He desires to speak to you on a personal level.*** God uses activities that you enjoy or skills that He's gifted you with as outlets for getting to know Him more. For example, I love to write. I enjoy all kinds of writing, but I really love to produce poetry and spoken word. My passion for writing has become one of the main ways I am able to get to know God better. When I write, I spend time in prayer and meditation on God's Word, and He has used those times to speak to me and teach me things in a unique way.

If you have not already discovered a unique way that God connects with you, I encourage you to pray about it. Maybe it's through singing, playing an instrument, doing art, dance, or sports. Or, maybe you are able to really get to know God through something like serving others, encouraging others, teaching people, helping, or caring for those around you. Whatever it is, continue in it and ask God to reveal more of Himself to you through it!

Spending time in God's Word:

Did you know that God wrote a love letter to you? That's right – that's exactly what the Bible is! So if you want to hear God's voice, studying His love letter to you is a great place to start!

When Jesus was being tempted by the devil in the wilderness, He told the devil that "man shall not live by bread alone, but by every word that comes from the mouth of God." (Matthew 4:4)

Remember that God has given us His Word through the Bible. When you read Scripture, He will be faithful to teach you through it.

Sometimes it is helpful for me to set up a schedule of when I'm going to read my Bible. I'd encourage you to try this. Set aside a time when you know you won't have any distractions. I like to go through certain books, one at a time. Find whatever works best for you. If you want to plan to read a certain book and read one chapter of that book every day, that's awesome! If you want to read a random Psalm during your quiet time, that's awesome too! You could even find a friend or group of friends who will read the same thing as you and then you could talk about it together. You and your friend could discuss what God taught each of you through what you read.

However you choose to go about reading the Bible, remember to keep an open mind and an open heart. Rid yourself of distractions so that you can focus on what you're learning. This will allow you to better understand what you're reading and will make it easier to pick up on the things God is trying to teach you through His Word.

Listening to His voice:

The best way to hear God is simply to listen. Praying to God is awesome, but just like any true friend, *God desires to have a two way conversation with you!* And keep in mind that truly listening to God requires us to have a willing and open heart because sometimes God speaks to us in unexpected ways.

I like to think of the story of Elijah on Mount Horeb in 1 Kings 19:11-13. The passage says this: "...a great and powerful wind tore the mountains apart and shattered the rocks before the LORD but the LORD was not in the wind. After the wind there was an earthquake, but the LORD was not in the earthquake. After the earthquake came a fire, but the LORD was not in the fire. And after the fire came a gentle whisper. When Elijah heard it, he pulled his cloak over his face and went out and stood at the mouth of the cave..."

Elijah might have expected to hear his mighty God through the wind, earthquake, or fire, but instead God spoke to him through a gentle whisper. Elijah knew God was speaking through the gentle whisper because he was listening, he was ready, and he was wanting to hear God.

It can be hard to take time to be still and listen for what God is trying to say to us because life can be very busy. There are constant distractions that seem to demand our attention. What we need to ask ourselves is, *"**Am I willing to sacrifice part of my day to listen to what my Savior wants to tell me?**"*

Since it's rare that God speaks audibly to us (though He can speak audibly to us if He chooses to), we have to tune our hearts to listen for God's still, small voice. God may speak to you through your pastor, friends, family, scripture, an event that takes place, etc. So, listen not only with your ears, but listen with your eyes and with your heart. That simply requires being aware of what's going on around you because you never know when or how God is going to teach you something new. So listen up!

3. How do I know when it's God's voice?

- *Are you ever confused about what you think you're hearing?*

This is still something that I am learning on a daily basis, so I'm going to share with you what God has taught me so far on my journey.

First of all, God will never tell us something that is contradictory to scripture. So knowing God's Word comes in handy when you are trying to discern His voice. If you feel like God is telling you to do something, but it's obviously contradictory to scripture, then it's not from God. It's always a good idea to check with a pastor or mentor that you trust and get their opinion because it may also be that you're misunderstanding a passage of scripture.

Having older Christian mentors in your life, who you can trust, is a great idea when it comes to trying to determine whether or not God is telling you something. The body of Christ is meant to work together and help each other. Consulting other believers is always a good idea when you're questioning whether or not you're hearing God correctly.

Remember that God has given you the Holy Spirit to direct and guide you. If you feel like God is telling you to do something, but you're not 100% positive, **pray about it and ask God to give you a supernatural peace about it if it's from Him**. You may still feel nervous going into it, but if it's from God, the Holy Spirit will give you a peace about what's happening.

Prayer is the most powerful tool we have in determining whether or not we're hearing from God. If you're confused about whether God is telling you something or not, the best thing to do is simply ask Him about it! Pray and listen, and He will provide you with clarity when you seek Him.

Pray:

Almighty God,

I want to be close to You.

I want to hear Your still, small voice.

So Lord, I am drawing near to You.

Thank You that You've promised that You will draw near to me.

Thank You for being there whenever I seek You.

My desire is to know You more every day.

Reveal Yourself to me in new ways and teach me more about Your character.

Help me to open up my heart to listen to You.

God, as I study Your Word I ask that You teach me new things.

I continue to chase after You, my King, because I desire You above all else.

Teach me to know Your voice.

Thank You for speaking to me in such a personal way.

Thank You for wanting to have a friendship with me.

Amen.

Take a few minutes right now to get rid of any distractions that are currently clouding your mind. Ask God to speak to you. Thank Him for the ability to have a friendship with Him. When you're done praying, take a few minutes to just sit and listen. Don't let the busy pace of life distract you. Just be still and know that He is God (Psalm 46:10). Open up your heart to hear His gentle whisper.

<u>Chapter 8: The Love of God</u>

What does God's love look like? What should our love look like?

Learn:

"A new commandment I give to you, that you love one another: just as I have loved you, you also are to love one another. By this all people will know that you are my disciples, if you have love for one another." (John 13:34-35)

When I read these verses, three main points stick out to me. First, Jesus is calling us to love each other. Secondly, we are supposed to love like He's loved us. And lastly, when we love others with a Godly love, it will be clear to the world that we are followers of God.

Every human being has the capacity to love. Why? Because every person is created in the image of God and "God is love" (Genesis 1:27, 1 John 4:8). But see, we live in a fallen world and so we have corrupted the idea of love. Many people "love" out of greed or selfishness when in reality that is the exact opposite of what love really is. Our culture has taken the word "love" and has abused it so much that it's hard for us to even determine its core meaning. But thankfully, the Bible offers us a clear description of true, pure, Godly love... It's when we truly love like God has loved us that things begin to change and blind eyes are opened.

In 1 Corinthians 13: 4-8, 13 Paul paints us a beautiful picture of what love truly is. He says, "Love is patient and kind; love does not envy or boast; it is not arrogant or rude. It does not insist on its own way; it is not irritable or resentful; it does not rejoice at wrong doing, but rejoices with the truth. Love bears all things, believes all things, hopes all things, endures all things. Love never ends. ... So now faith, hope, and love abide, these three; but the greatest of these is love."

As I read through this description, I can't help but think of all the times I have *not* been patient, and that I *have* been prideful, rude, irritable, and so on. And then I think of the one who came and lived out that list above – and did it perfectly. Did you catch that? Jesus fulfilled each of these things *perfectly*. ***He first loved us in all of these ways and then called us to go and love others in the same way.***

God's love for us is so simple and yet, so indescribable. It is not something that is overly complicated, but at the same time, it leaves us speechless. It's hard for us to wrap our minds around the concept of God's love because it is so perfect in its nature and it's so far from who we are and how we act in our natural flesh. It can be difficult to grasp because ***His love is a sacrificial love***. Our

God's love for us is one of the key distinctions between Him and the gods of other religions. His loving sacrifice very clearly demonstrates His desire to have us for His own. It proves to us that He wants us to know Him on an intimate level. The sacrificial love of God is described perfectly in what is probably the most famous Bible verse.

In John 3:16 John says, *"For God so loved the world*, that he gave his only Son, that whoever believes in him should not perish but have eternal life."

This verse is so well known that the incredible love and sacrifice God showed the world is often looked over or taken for granted. God *loved* and because He loved, He *gave…* and because He gave, we are now capable of *receiving eternal life.* How amazing! Now God calls us to go and love others so that they might see Him through us.

In order to love others like God loves, we must first be in love with God ourselves. What does this mean? What I mean by "being in love with God" is simply having a personal relationship with Him. When you spend a lot of time with Him and He is your best friend, being in love with Him comes naturally.

Here is what I have found – *the more I fall in love with Jesus, the easier and more natural it becomes to love others.* We will never know what it looks like to be fully in love with God here on earth; but every day is a learning process and there's something exciting about that process. ***Every day is a new opportunity to learn more about God's love, to fall further in love with Him, and to show His love to those around us.***

Act:

The Bible has a lot to say about *who* we should love and *how* we should love. It tells us that we are to love God, love our neighbors, and even love our enemies. Love is a verb and we must choose daily whether we will act on it. We often fall short of showing love to those around us and when we fall short, we must look to God, whose very nature is love.

Why are we called to love? The Bible gives us a very simple answer to this question. **John tells us in 1 John 4:19 that "We love because he first loved us."**

God loves you. Because of this simple fact, you have been given the capacity to love others. ***His love for us is the drive behind the reason we love.*** He chose to love us first, and He didn't show just a small amount of love for us; in fact, He showed the greatest kind of love He could show. He didn't hold anything back when He gave Himself in your place.

"Greater love has no one than this, that someone lay down his life for his friends." (John 15:13)

God loved you first. He loved you with the greatest kind of love. Now you have to ask yourself: *What am I going to do with this love?* Please don't keep it to yourself. I'd like to challenge you to go and share His love with those around you. ***Will you choose to love because He first loved you?***

Loving God

- **"You shall love the Lord your God with all your heart and with all you soul and with all you mind." (Matthew 22:37)**
  - I talked about this verse quite a bit in chapter 5, but I think it's an important verse to bring up when talking about how we are to love God. ***God calls us to love Him with absolutely everything we are***. When we think about God's incredible, sacrificial love for us, our response should be to love Him in return with every ounce of our being. God did not hold back His love from us, and He does not want us to hold back our love for Him. Our lives are called to be a reflection of His sacrifice.
- **"Jesus answered him, 'If anyone loves me, he will keep my word, and my Father will love him, and will come to**

him and make our home with him. Whoever does not love me does not keep my words." (John 14:23-24)

- In this verse, Jesus is very straightforward. How can we show God that we love Him?...By obeying Him and keeping His word. This is another reason it is so important to study the Word of God. Every time I read my Bible, I become more aware of how God wants me to live, and I get a better picture of what it looks like to live as a reflection of Jesus. Studying God's Word and living out its truth is equivalent to expressing love for God. When we love God by keeping His word, He promises us that He will make His home with us.

- **"For this is the love of God, that we keep his commandments. And his commandments are not burdensome." (1 John 5:3)**

  - Again, it is emphasized that obeying God is a demonstration of our love for Him. But the greatest part is that God's commandments for us are not meant to burden us. God wants the best for His children; His goal is not to burden His creation with arbitrary commandments that we have to follow. Rather, the commandments that God has set in place for us are not burdensome because His "yoke is easy and His burden is light" (Matthew 11:30). And so, He calls us to obey Him in order to reflect our love for Him.

Loving Your Neighbor

- **Jesus says in Mark 12:31 "The second is this: 'You shall love your neighbor as yourself.' There is no other commandment greater than these."**

  - Jesus says this right after saying that you should love God with all of your heart, soul, mind, and strength. Loving your neighbor as yourself is obviously an extremely important command given by Jesus*. Loving others is an action that naturally comes from loving Christ.* What does loving others look like? Well, go back to the 1 Corinthians 13:4-8 passage that I referenced at the beginning of this chapter. Those few verses give us clear instructions as to what our love for our neighbor should look like. We should treat others in a way we would want to be treated (Luke 6:31). God calls us to love others with a patient, humble, and kind heart.

- **In Romans 13:8-10 Paul gives us a clearer understanding as to why it is so important to love our neighbors. He says, "Owe no one anything, except to love each other, for the one who loves another has fulfilled the law. For** the commandments, 'You shall not commit adultery, You shall not murder, You shall not steal, You shall not covet,' and any other commandment, are summed up in this word: 'You shall love your neighbor as yourself.' Love does no wrong to a neighbor; therefore love is the fulfilling of the law."

- Paul clearly identifies the importance of loving our neighbor when he points out the fact that if we love your neighbors, then we will not hurt them in any way because *love does no wrong to a neighbor.* If you love your neighbors, you will not murder them. If you love your neighbors, you will not cheat them, steal from them, lie to them, etc. If you love God, then you will have a heart to love those around you. If you love those around you, then you will serve them humbly just as Christ served you. And the Bible also tells us that it is through this love for others that the world will notice that we are followers of Christ. (John 13:35)

Loving Your Enemies

- **Jesus not only tells us to love our neighbors, but he also commands us to love our enemies. He tells us in Luke 6:27-28 "Love your enemies, do good to those who hate** you, bless those who curse you, pray for those who abuse you."

- Love your enemies. Jesus gives us this odd and very difficult command, but loving our enemies is definitely not something the world is encouraging us to do. In fact, the world tells us that we should seek revenge on our enemies and that we have the right to hate those who have wronged us. But God tells us the opposite. And get this...we are called, as children of God, not only to love our enemies, but to *do good* to them and to pray for them. A little later in this same passage of scripture, Jesus tells us why we should love our enemies.

- **Jesus says in Luke 6:35-36 "But love your enemies, and do good, and lend, expecting nothing in return, and your reward will be great, and you will be sons of the Most High, for he is kind to the ungrateful and the evil. Be merciful, even as your Father is merciful."**

  - Jesus doesn't ask us to love our enemies just for the fun of it. *He commands us to love those who are against us because He loves those who are against Him.* As God's children, we are called to be imitators of Him; a reflection of Him here on this earth (Ephesians 5:1). God is kind and merciful to all. In all believers' lives there was a point when they were an enemy of God, ungrateful, and stuck in their evil and sinful ways. But because of His great love, He had mercy on us and made a way for us to be saved. It is now our job as people who were once enemies of God, but are now friends of God, to display that love to those on this earth who are against us. God is a just God and will reward us for such love. Don't be misled by the world into believing that it is your right to take revenge on your enemies.

- **Paul tells us that it is not our job to take revenge on our enemies. He says in Romans 12:19-21, "Beloved, never avenge yourselves, but leave it to the wrath of God, for it is written, 'Vengeance is mine, I will repay, says the Lord.' To the contrary, 'if your enemy is hungry, feed him; if he is thirsty, give him something to drink…Do not be overcome by evil, but overcome evil with good."**
  - If you are battling with feeling like you have the right to avenge yourself, remember this scripture. Leave it in God's hands. Because He is a just God, He will punish evil in the days of judgment. Until then, love your enemies, care for them, pray for them, and leave everything else in God's hands. *Trying to overcome evil with more evil will only get you into a bigger*

mess. Rather, ***overcome evil with good*** because the last thing Satan wants to see is the powerful love of God at work in you.

Pray:

Heavenly Father,

I pray that You would fill me up with Your love.

Let me never forget or take for granted

the amazing and sacrificial love You have for me.

I am so grateful for Your love for me.

I ask that You continue to teach me how to love

those around me in a way that reflects You.

Lord, I want to grow deeper in my love for You every day.

Teach me to love my neighbors as well as my enemies

and remind me that I love because You first loved me.

I pray for those around me – I pray that You would bless them

and that You would help me to love them joyfully.

I pray for my enemies –

I pray that You would bless them and guide them.

Let them see Your love through me.

Thank You that You give me the strength

to overcome evil with good through Your love.

Thank You for setting the ultimate example of love for us.

I love you, Lord.

Amen.

I encourage you right now to just sit quietly and think about God's love for you. Ponder the sacrifice He made for you, how He flawlessly demonstrated perfect love. Let Him know how grateful you are for His amazing love. Also, think about yourself – do you love others in a way that reflects Christ's love? Pray that God would continue to shape your heart so that you can be a more accurate reflection of Him.

<u>Chapter 9: Taking In and Giving Out</u>

What are you going to do with what Christ has given you?

Learn:

Imagine yourself outside on a hot summer's day. You are with a few friends and they're all getting very thirsty. You have a pitcher that's been filled with cold water and you see that your friends are in need of a drink. Would you pour out cups of water and give them to your thirsty friends or would you keep the water all to yourself? Would you be afraid that your pitcher would not be refilled? Hopefully your answer is that you would pour a cup of water for your friends, that you wouldn't withhold that much needed drink from them because of a fear of running out of water.

As Christians, we have been given a priceless gift; we have experienced and have access to the life giving water of Christ. But so often we stand with our pitcher of water and do nothing with it even though there are people all around us who are in need of a drink. We become afraid of pouring out our pitcher because we think that we will then be empty. So often we are held back by fear. What we need to realize is that *in order to continuously be*

poured into, we need to continuously be pouring out. God fills you up, you pour out onto others, God fills you up, you pour out onto others…and so the cycle continues. God will never leave your pitcher empty. In fact, the more you pour out, the more God will pour into you.

Think of yourself as the pitcher – God's vessel. Now imagine the water being your knowledge of the gospel and your life changing experience of knowing God personally. The water could also include the various gifts, talents, energy and time that God has given you. Every time you use those gifts in service for others and every time you share the truth that you know in order to expand God's kingdom, you are pouring out your water. Spending time with God and being filled with his Spirit is how your pitcher gets full again. Is it coming together now in your mind?

Now, I am *not* saying to go crazy and volunteer for every single opportunity that comes your way. God has called us to be wise with our time and also to take time to rest. What I *am* saying is that we should not be frugal when it comes to pouring out service in our daily lives. We are not called to sit and watch as the people around us suffer and are in desperate need of a "drink." But at the same time, we are also not the ones who are capable of saving people - no matter how much of ourselves we give. And so, it's important to find a healthy balance and to simply give freely because Christ has freely poured into us.

Paul says in Galatians 6:7-10, "Whatever one sows, that will he also reap. For the one who sows to his own flesh will from the flesh reap corruption, but the one who sows to the Spirit will from the Spirit reap eternal life. And let us not grow weary of doing good, for in due season we will reap, if we do not give up. So then, as we have opportunity, let us do good to everyone and especially to those who are of the household of faith."

In order to "sow to the Spirit" we first need to take in (or be filled with) the Spirit. As Christians, the Spirit of God lives and dwells in us. We need to "keep in step with the Spirit" by growing in the fruits of the Spirit and by not falling to temptation and to the desires of the flesh (Galatians 5:25). As we are filled by the ways of the Spirit, we are then called to give back by sowing. So, what we sow, or give out, will be based on what we take in. And what we sow will not be overlooked; we will reap whatever we have sown.

We have been given a priceless gift. We have taken in the living water of Christ, and it is now our job to give back out by sharing this wonderful truth with those around us. *With every opportunity we get to give or serve, we should be offering ourselves – unafraid of running dry – because we know we serve a God who is faithful to fill us up again.* If we sow to the Spirit, we will reap from the Spirit and so the cycle is endless.

Jesus says in Luke 6:38, "Give, and it will be given to you. Good measure, pressed down, shaken together, running over, will be put into your lap. For with the measure you use it will be measured back to you."

Jesus knows what's best for us. He knows that it is better for us to give not only because it will benefit others, but also because it will benefit us. In this verse, we can clearly see *the cycle of God's economy*. We give and it is given back to us, and so we give more and we are blessed again. This does not mean that when we give, God will then make us rich. Rather, as we give (of our money, time, talents, etc.) in order to bless those around us, God will be faithful to provide for us and will bless us for blessing others. We are His children, and He will always provide what we need.

Jesus describes how He will provide for us when we give by saying **"good measure, pressed down, shaken together, running over, will be put into your lap."** Here He is referring to grain or possibly some other type of food to give an illustration and to make a point. He's describing how a large amount of grain would be "pressed down" or crushed up in order to fit more compactly into a container. It would then be shaken to settle the crushed pieces, creating even more space. The container would be so filled with the grain that it would run over into the person's lap. This is the comparison Jesus uses in order to describe how He will provide for us when we give. It was certainly a culturally and historically clear illustration for the people living in his day, and it is still a powerful visual image for us now.

Act:

Giving can take on many different forms. We can give of our money, our time, and our talents. We can give advice and we can give a listening ear. But most importantly, we can give people the truth of the gospel which is the most priceless gift of all. No matter what we're giving, it's always important to remember that we cannot give salvation; only Christ can give that. But, through the various ways we give we can lead people and position them to receive salvation from Christ. And remember, we don't need to be afraid or hesitant to give because God is faithful to fill us back up and provide for us. ***Not only does He promise to fill our cups, but He promises to fill us to overflowing.***
Taking In:

In order to receive or take in more of Christ (which is essential for being able to pour out more of Him), you must first empty yourself of things that do not please God. This is not something that can be done once, but rather is a constant process of surrendering all that you are to Him, day after day.

Paul says this in 2 Timothy 2:21: "Therefore, if anyone cleanses himself from what is dishonorable, he will be a vessel for honorable use, set apart as holy, useful to the master of house, ready for every good work."

Cleansing ourselves of dishonorable things is crucial when it comes to being filled with Christ because his holiness cannot mix with what is dishonorable. We simply cannot live half committed to the world and half committed to Christ. We must be 100% sold out to one of them. So, if we desire to be used by God, we must daily cleanse ourselves in order to be a "vessel for honorable use." We will then be "ready for every good work," we'll be able to be filled with more of Christ and, therefore, we'll be able to pour out more of ourselves (and ultimately, more of Him) onto those we serve.

Giving Out:

"One gives freely, yet grows all the richer; another withholds what he should give, and only suffers want. Whoever brings blessing will be enriched, and one who waters will himself be watered." – Proverbs 11:24-25

God has blessed us each immensely and holding back what He has given us will do us no good. He has given us many gifts and talents and has given them for specific reasons. Through giving of what God has blessed us with, we in return will be blessed. When you give your time or you share a talent God has given you for His glory, God will see what you give out and will fill you in a greater way. Remember the purpose of it all: We are filled up so that we might pour out in return.

Peter also explains the importance of giving what we have received. In 1 Peter 4:10-11 he says, "As each has received a gift, use it to serve one another, as good stewards of God's varied grace: whoever speaks, as one who speaks oracles of God; whoever serves, as one who serves by the strength that God supplies – in order that in everything God may be glorified through Jesus Christ. To him belong the glory and dominion forever and ever. Amen."

We have all received various gifts from God for a reason – to put them to use. If you don't know what you are gifted in, pray that God would reveal it to you. As you discover your different gifts, put them to use in your daily life. If you are an encourager, then encourage the people around you on a daily basis. If you have a heart to serve with practical assistance, find ways in your community, school, or church that you could offer a helpful hand. If you are gifted at singing, then look for opportunities to lead worship or encourage others through songs you write. Everyone is gifted in different ways, and there are endless opportunities to "give out" by putting those gifts to use.

As you discover how to best utilize your gifts, you'll find that the more you give out the more God will fill you up. You will become more and more excited to then give out again. I have found that ***people are most joyful and most fulfilled when they are in the midst of walking in what God has created them to do.*** You don't have to be afraid that if you freely pour out the love of Christ onto people that you might somehow eventually run dry. You can rest assured in the fact that as you continue to pour out God's love in various ways, God is faithful to fill you back up to the point of overflowing!

As Christians, our ultimate goal is to bring glory to God. We should be motivated to give of our time, energy, gifts and resources simply because we long to honor God in all that we do. We should expect nothing in return because we "received without paying" and so we should "give without pay" (Matthew 10:8). We should give, trusting God that He will provide for our needs. ***We are filled by God so that we can empty out what He gives us onto those around us... so that He might fill us up again.***

Think back to the illustration at the beginning of this chapter. Imagine yourself with a cold pitcher of water on a hot day. Your friends are there and are in need of a drink. Will you choose to keep the water all to yourself? Will you hesitate in fear that your pitcher will not be refilled? Or, will you *choose to give*, expecting nothing in return but trusting that God will fill your pitcher to overflowing over and over again?

Pray:

Lord,

I surrender all that I am to You.

Take me, and cleanse me so that I might be of use to You.

Thank You for the priceless gift that You've given me.

Open my eyes to the opportunities around me to pour out Your love on others.

Thank You that I can rest assured

that You will fill me up when I pour myself out for You.

Help me to keep in step with the Spirit so that I might sow of the Spirit.

Give me boldness to live my life for You.

Show me the areas in which You have gifted me

and help me to put them to use for You.

Thank You for blessing me and for pouring into me.

I will freely give what You have blessed me with so that others might see Your goodness.

I do all that I do to bring You glory and honor.

Thank You for Your unending faithfulness to me.

Fill me up so that I might be poured out.

Amen.

I encourage you now to take a moment and thank God for all that He's done for you. If you are not sure how God has gifted you, ask Him now to reveal to you that gift. Ask Him for opportunities to serve others. Thank Him for how He is so faithful to fill you and rest assured in that truth.

Chapter 10: Being Focused & Staying Motivated

How can you stay focused on Christ in the midst of life's chaos?
What is your source of motivation?

Learn:

Staying focused and motivated can prove to be very difficult tasks on a day-to-day basis. ***With so many distractions in our culture and in today's high-speed world, it becomes very easy to get sidetracked.*** When people become unfocused and unmotivated, they often fall into the traps of procrastination and laziness as well...and it shows in their daily lives. For example, let's say you have a big project due in a week for school or for work. If you are not focused on the project at hand and are unmotivated to finish it, most likely you will wait until the last minute to do it. This could lead to you handing in a messy, poorly done assignment.

We can all admit that there have been times in our daily lives when we haven't been able to focus on the task at hand or have been unmotivated to complete a task. But we must be very careful not to carry a mindset of procrastination and laziness into our spiritual lives; doing so can be very dangerous. Christ has given us the greatest task of all, and He tells us that in order to accomplish it we will need to focus on Him and keep each other motivated to press on.

"Therefore, since we are surrounded by so great a cloud of witnesses, let us lay aside every weight, and sin which clings so closely, and let us run with endurance the race that is set before us, *looking to Jesus*, the founder and perfecter of our faith, who for the joy that was set before him endured the cross, despising the shame, and is seated at the right hand of the throne of God." – Hebrews 12:1-2

God has set a great race before us. It's a race down the straight and narrow path which leads to life (Matthew 7:14). He does not promise us that the race will be easy; in fact, He tells us that we will face tribulation. But He also tells us to take heart because He has already overcome the world (John 16:33). Running this race with endurance means that we will need to be focused. ***Through the highs and the lows of life, we need to be looking to Jesus, focused on Him, in order to keep moving forward.*** It's when our focus shifts from Christ that we begin to slip and feel distant from Him and when our focus is not on Jesus, we will not be able to move forward...and moving forward is an essential piece to finishing the race.

Being motivated to run is also a very important aspect of the race. Hebrews 12:2 tells us that Jesus endured the cross "for the joy that was set before Him." Jesus came to this earth and ran His race with endurance because He was focused and motivated. He was focused on the task His Father had set before Him, which was to endure the cross to pay for our sins. He was motivated to obey His Father and He was motivated by the reward of buying us back.

Jesus set the ultimate example for us of what it looks like to run the race with focus and motivation. He faced temptations of every kind, yet He kept His focus on the task His Father had set before Him (Hebrews 4:15). His holy motivation was more powerful than any temptation to give up. Now He calls us to run the race and continue the mission.

Act:

You have control over what you focus on and what you allow to motivate you. For the most part, you are capable of choosing the things you look at, the things you listen to, activities you partake in, and who you spend your time with. ***The daily choices you make impact what you are ultimately focusing your time and energy on. What you are focusing on then becomes your ultimate source of motivation.*** And so we must be very careful and selective about what we choose to focus our attention on. We must also be mindful of who or what we allow to motivate us.

Staying Focused

Staying focused on Christ can be very difficult in the midst of our chaotic world. I want to share with you some simple methods found in scripture that you can use to stay focused on Christ in your daily life.

1. Don't worry.

Jesus says, "Do not be anxious about your life, what you will eat or what you will drink, nor about your body, what you will put on. Is not life more than food, and the body more than clothing? Look at the birds of the air: they neither sow nor reap nor gather into barns, and yet your heavenly Father feeds them. Are you not of more value than they? …But seek first the kingdom of God and his righteousness, and all these things will be added to you." – Matthew 6:25-26, 33

- In order to focus on Jesus, you have to trust Him. If you are constantly worrying about having enough food in the house, or worrying about how your body looks, or if you have clothes of the latest fashion, then you are causing your focus to drift away from Him. When you worry about something, the majority of your time and energy is spent *focusing on that thing*. Jesus tells us that He knows our needs. He reminds us that He provides for the birds that are of less value than us. ***Our focus needs to first and foremost be on the kingdom of God.*** Jesus says that when we focus our attention **first** on the kingdom of God, "then all these things will be added to us." God is faithful to provide for us so there is no need to worry. In fact, the only thing worrying will accomplish is to hinder you from running the race with endurance, so set your mind on kingdom things.

2. Do NOT befriend the world.

James advises us in James 4:4 by saying, "Do you not know that friendship with the world is enmity with God? Therefore whoever wishes to be a friend of the world makes himself an enemy of God."

- Trying to be "friends" with the world, or following after the ways of the world is a recipe for disaster if you are also trying to follow after Jesus. It would be quite a challenge to focus all of your attention and passion on serving God if He were your enemy. In fact, it is impossible to be friends with both God and the world. If your desire is to truly set your focus of Jesus and run the race with endurance, then you must be *in* the world, but not *of* it. Ask yourself these questions: *Do I have a better friendship with this world or with Jesus? Who has captivated my full attention – the world or Jesus"* Every day, we need to renew our minds so that we will not be conformed to the ways of the world, but rather be daily transformed to look more like Christ (Romans 12:2). Be sure to "set your mind on things that are above, not on things that are on the earth" (Colossians 3:2).

3. Use a filter.

Paul says in Philippians 4:8, "Finally, brothers, whatever is true, whatever is honorable, whatever is just, whatever is pure, whatever is lovely, whatever is commendable, if there is any excellence, if there is anything worthy of praise, think about these things."

- Staying focused on Christ has a lot to do with what we choose to fill our minds with. I find it interesting that Paul tells us to **think** about such things. We are constantly thinking, constantly talking to ourselves in a sense. Filtering what we audibly say and what we physically do is one thing. This tends to be easier because these are the things that others around us can clearly hear and see. But filtering our thoughts is different. The people around us can't see or hear our thoughts and so it's often easier for us to avoid filtering that internal conversation that only we (and God) know about. But the reality is that our thoughts have huge effect on our lives. For example, if you are constantly thinking negatively about yourself, sooner or later you're going to believe those negative things to be true. And in the same way, if you are constantly thinking about dishonorable, impure, negative, unkind things, then sooner or later that will show through your actions and words. ***Those thoughts will become habitual and the longer you think on them, the harder it will be to break that habit.*** When our thoughts are on such dishonorable things, then they cannot also be on Christ. The list of virtuous qualities that Paul gives us in the verse above will have limited space in a mind that is focused elsewhere.

- For these reasons, it becomes extremely important to filter your thoughts. If you find your mind drifting to think on things that are the opposite of this list given by Paul...stop. Stop yourself as soon as you realize it. You have control over your thoughts. Start praying that God would remove those things from your mind. Memorize scripture and say it to yourself. When my mind starts to wander, I like to sing worship songs. Regardless of what form it comes in (music, written word, through time in prayer), the truth of God is the key ingredient to being able to control our thoughts. When we are truly focused on Him, it will show through all other aspects of our lives.

Staying Motivated

Staying motivated is also extremely important when it comes to running the race that's been set before us. Often times, the more focused we are on the task at hand the more motivated we become. But sometimes staying motivated on our own can be difficult. This is where the family of God comes into play. It's so important to have strong believers in your life who are there to keep you accountable and to motivate you to keep running. If you want to obey God and draw closer to Him, it's also important to remember that your main source of motivation should come from God himself.

1. Others as a source of motivation

"And let us consider how to stir up one another to love and good works, not neglecting to meet together, as is the habit of some, but encouraging one another, and all the more as you see the Day drawing near." – Hebrews 10:24-25

- We are a family in Christ and are meant to encourage one another. It is essential to have other believers in your life who are there for you to listen to you, to love you, to talk with you, and to motivate you... Not only should you have others in your life who are encouragers for you, but you should also look to *be* that person for others as well. Be someone who loves like Christ loves and is there to encourage and motivate the believers around you.

2. Christ (and His promises) as a source of motivation

"Set your mind on things that are above, not on things that are on earth. For you have died, and your life is hidden with Christ in God. When Christ who is your life appears, then you also will appear with him in glory." – Colossians 3:2-4

- When you are focused on kingdom things, your motivation will then come from desiring God. As you run your race, allow God to be your ultimate source of motivation and continue running with endurance, remembering that He has promised to return. Your life is hidden in Him and so when He returns you "will appear with him in glory." A day is coming when Christ will come again and judge the world. If you've been redeemed by His blood, then God will no longer see your past mistakes, but rather will see His Son, Jesus, alive in you. Because of His sacrifice, you will be able to enter into heavenly eternity with God. What an amazing motivator to keep our eyes locked on Him! If you ever feel your focus shifting away from Christ or you are feeling unmotivated to continue pursuing Him, remember God's love for you. Remember the sacrifice Jesus made in order to buy you back and allow that to motivate you to keep running the race with endurance.

Pray:

Lord,

Thank You for the sacrifice You made for me.

Help me to run the race You've set before me and keep me focused on You.

Lord, I want You to be my ultimate source of motivation.

Thank You for placing other believers around me to also motivate me.

I pray that I too would be a source of encouragement for others.

Help me not to worry, but to trust in You.

I do not want to be conformed to the ways of this world.

I give myself to You so that You can transform me to be more like You.

I also ask that You purify my thoughts.

Help me to think on things that are pleasing to You.

I cannot thank You enough for all that You've done for me.

I will choose to run this race, focused on You and motivated by Your promises.

I love You, Lord.

Amen.

Take a moment to think about your life's main focus. Maybe there are some things that you need to hand over to God that have been getting in the way of you being able to focus fully on Him. Also, think about what motivates you to keep running. Ask God to be that source of motivation and to send others into your life to encourage you as well. Thank Him for the sacrifice He made so that you have a chance to be able to run to Him.

End Thoughts:

I hope that through reading this devotional, you were able to learn and grow in your relationship with Jesus. I certainly do not put into practice all the topics within this book perfectly, but they are all topics that I have been motivated to grow in. My prayer is that you are encouraged and excited to live your life whole heartedly for Jesus. He deserves it all!

Never forget that living life with Jesus is a crazy, awesome adventure! You are able to walk in victory every day because He has already won the victory for you. It's all about daily surrender and daily pursuit of Him. Allow His Spirit to penetrate your very being; allow Him to have full control over your life. My prayer for you is that you come to recognize the incredible, unconditional love of the Father's heart and that you allow that love to transform your life.

My last thought for you is this: be bold! Wherever you are, be bold for Him. We must let His light shine *through* us, and let His love pour *out* of us because He is so worthy of all that we are!

44700852R00063

Made in the USA
Middletown, DE
14 June 2017